Mini Stories from the Fens

AN AREA like the Fens is bound to be rich in stories. Happily, a century or more ago, someone, somewhere, the possessor of a receptive mind, happened to be conveniently placed to observe, memorise and make notes when something startling or unusual occurred; or listened to a sage relate his or her experiences and share knowledge of things and events of yesteryear. Some of these strange and interesting anecdotes first appeared in printer's ink more than a hundred years ago; some originators passed on their memories verbally. There are several sources concerned with this collection of mini-stories and I see no reason to doubt the authenticity of them.

That they had their origin in the Fens, an environment with which I am well acquainted, fills me with no great surprise. I know that Fenland, so full of mystery, is amply filled with historical niceties, legends and stirring events born of the environment, the people and magnitude of its famous history which few other rural areas can offer. This little book, crammed with anecdotes can merely scratch the surface, for beyond these pages there must be hundreds of stories etched in the depths of countless minds, as well as those on yellowed pieces of paper wedged into attics, boxes, drawers and spaces seldom opened to the light of day. In this revised edition, the author adds a few more stories which came his way for he has an insatiable nose for the past! He has also added different illustrations for better effect as befits so rural an area as the Fens.

Reference Material

The Sunday Magazine (1897); Fenland Notes and Queries (1892–1900); Records of a Fen Parish; Gardiner's History of Wisbech; The Chronica Majora; and numerous accumulated notes an

G000299360

ISBN 0 901680 19 2   *Revised 1992*   (

Published by the author, 28 St. Peter's Road, March, Cambridgeshire. PE15 9NA
Tel: (0354) 57286

Printed by David J. Richards, Commercial Printers and Stationers,
1 West Park Street, Chatteris, Cambridgeshire. PE16 6AH
Tel: (0354) 692947.

Old time
Fen gentleman

Secrets of Whittlesey Mere

Whittlesey Mere formed a very shallow fresh water lake – the largest in southern England. It varied in depth between two and four feet and covered 3,000 acres. The mere was the last survivor of many similar meres and was finally sucked away in 1850 by the country's first centrifugal pump to the regret of many. Whittlesey Mere provided a prolific livelihood to Fenmen and was famous for its eels and many varieties of fish and waterfowl. Its dried bed of mud yielded a boat 27 feet long by four-and-a-half feet wide crudely hewn in one piece and filled with acorns and nuts and a silver censer case and ornaments which had belonged to Ramsey abbey.

The mere was used by the monks of Ramsey, Sawtry and Peterborough, those great monastic institutions possessing several grants in the Fens including fisheries. Many months passed before the drained surface of Whittlesey Mere would bear a man's weight. When it had finally dried out and great fissures appeared over its surface, the roots of water lilies and other plants could be clearly seen. An iron post from the Great Exhibition calibrated in feet and inches was driven into the solid clay. In 1875 eight feet two inches of the post was exposed through peat shrinkage and in 1992 at least as much again has emerged from the ground.

Sank into the Mere

During the drainage era a great many hazards were experienced in the Fens. A young lad who lived at Holme set out on one particular Sunday in 1851 to pursue his task as a bird scarer at Holme Fen. Around the drained bed of Whittlesey Mere was an area known as the reed shore, a source of revenue to its proprietors and very extensive, reaching anything between a quarter of a mile to half a mile into the drained mere. The reeds were exceedingly tall, some 14 feet upwards. If anyone ventured into this mass he was lost to sight. The boy wandered away from his safe position in the fen, got round by the reed shore and stepped into the dried bed of the mere. No sooner had he done so he began to sink and could not extricate himself, although he was only a yard from firm ground. Inch by inch he sank and quite expected the mud to engulf his head when at last his feet touched clay and he stopped sinking with the mud at his arm pits.

It was then half past three, confirmed in the boy's ears by Conington church clock. He could hear trains on the Great Northern railway line and kept shouting for help but to no avail, no-one ever passing so near to the treacherous bed of the lake. The lad spent an uncomfortable night, but while held fast he was not overcome by fatigue or cold, the mud shielding him from the cold air. The boy remained awake and sensible for the whole of the night, counting the time by the Conington clock. Next morning he could see a few fen labourers afar off but could not make them hear. Unable to make a sound, he heard at about 10 o'clock a man on the opposite side of the reed bed. Then the worker moved away and the boy thought he was doomed. Another half hour passed and he heard someone pushing through the reeds. In an unbelievable providential way the man's feet were guided right up to the boy's head and shoulders.

With the utmost difficulty the man managed to pull him out and carried him through the reed shore to the firm ground. Having spent 19 hours in the mud the boy was paralysed with cold and could not speak. His rescuer, a Holme man, carried him home to his parents who had thought that he was staying for the night with his grandmother at Sawtry. After acutely feeling the effects of his ordeal for two days the lad was declared fit and well by a Stilton surgeon and returned to school.

The Wet Droves

Years ago Fen droveways were little more than rutted earthy tracks. They appeared quite beautiful in summer months, being covered with all sorts of weeds, mossy greens, forget-me-nots and the pink or lesser cranesbill as well as numerous trailing plants. Came winter and the droves had turned into quagmires. Some were practically impassable and carts sank up to their axles in mud. An old Fen folklore has it that one man met another along one of the wet droves and enquired of him if he had seen a hat. "Naw," the other said. "I am not so much concerned about that," said the first, "but there is a man under the hat and a horse beneath him. If I find the hat I find them all!"

Where's that Horse?

A similar story existed at Doddington. Early one morning in the middle of the 19th century a man was seen cautiously feeling his way around the perimeter of a newly-drained field. A passer-by known to him shouted "Hey! What are you looking for?" His friend, keeping one eye on the squelchy surface, testing each step he made, replied: "There was a horse here this morning!" Even in our own age it is not uncommon for Fenland firemen to be called to a distressed beast which had ventured too far in mud to drink at a pond or had wandered into the mud on the side of a drain.

Fenland's Wind Engines

The wind engine was the earliest form of drainage machine. It looked almost identical to a windmill but had water scoops instead of stones for grinding corn. Water confined to the network of Fen rivers and drains was drawn from one engine to another and finally lifted into the main drain. The engines existed in their hundreds and presented a graceful sight. As far as the eye could see as many as forty might be idling away in the breeze. What a pity that not one remains, except the little wind engine on Wicken Fen Nature Reserve.

The engines were sluggish and unreliable as they depended upon a breeze. They were not economical to maintain (nor was the steam engines which succeeded them). "You see, master", said an old engine man to a former rector of March St. Wendreda's church, "she (the wind engine) was going all winter when she could, but the water all ran back again. It couldn't get away and often enough there was no wind for weeks. That's how the land came to be drowned. But bless you; 'tis all altered now. With this steam they can drain every drop out of the land and the rivers are always on the move".

Wind engines (see front cover) were constantly under repair. Their swiftly revolving sails were particularly vulnerable to wear and tear. The oak towers stood 40 feet high and were topped with a huge oak cap which could be turned into the wind. They had brick foundations but the rest was wood which was prone to damage. That was how it had to be as an heavier structure would have sunk into the river bank. The sails were 36 feet long and six or seven feet broad. The engine consisted of a few squared beams and massive cogwheels. The principal beam stood vertically within the structure, geared to the axle in the cap and the bottom end geared to the huge water wheel which was usually 30 feet in diameter and studded with boards which splashed water from the lower level of dykes to the higher level of the main drains. The keeper took up his abode in the winter, residing with his family in the noisy basement of the tower, a cramped space filled with the creaking of the engine as it went about its task.

The engine man had to turn the huge cap into the breeze with the aid of a chain and windlass. In the event of adverse weather he had to gather the canvas from the sails. Any reckless handling may cause the great sails to snap off like a carrot for which the engine man would be called sharply to account before irate commissioners – Fen farmers and landlords that knew the nature of things. The engine man undertook a dangerous task, the sails sweeping as low as two feet from the ground. When a person left the tower he had to dodge the

the flailing sails descending as little as two feet from the ground. This was more obvious when the sails swooped down a few feet from the door. An old time writer observed that the engine keeper's children ran in and out of the tower quite oblivious to the sails which somehow they avoided. The wind engines were usually empty for most part of the summer, the engine keeper generally employed in roding the ditches. He received the call to man the engine from Michaelmas onwards and he and his family vacated the tied cottage for a season in the creaking old engine tower. These places were the homes of a tough breed of people born and bred in a relentless environment.

Witchcraft in the Fens

Not surprisingly, in the distant past the Fens were riddled with superstition. When an old house was being demolished there was discovered beneath the hearth a low, flat-bottomed glass bottle. In it were several pins stuck to a dark substance. These were intended as a charm to keep evil spirits at bay. The dark substance was supposed to be a pigeon's heart . . . a sad reflection of a medieval custom which persisted in the Fens for many centuries.

As late as 1903 a Bottisham man who owned horses believed the animals were bewitched. He obtained from a "wise man" a countervailing charm in the form of compounded horseshoes with nails and iron fillings. After drinking the concoction one of the horses died. Ah, well!

One of the oldest Fen superstitions was that known as the Spidery Cure. If a person was suffering from the ague it was customary to take a spider and place it alive in a bag, then hang it around the patient's neck. This ancient custom was practiced by poor and rich alike – by the ignorant as well as the enlightened. Oddly enough it is recorded that many people were cured. Elias Ashmole wrote in his diary in 1681: "I took a spider this morning, a good dose of elixir and hung three spiders about my neck and they drove the plague away. Deo gratis". Perhaps it was the elixir! Sometimes the insects were carefully wrapped in a piece of pastry and swallowed alive!

Perhaps the method employed to cure a cancerous swelling in days gone by defies imagination more than any other, especially as it was carried out at the end of the 19th century. It was believed that to induce a painful gathering, such as a wen, to disappear it could be soothed away by stroking it with the hand of a corpse. This was considered to be even more effective if the body was that of a person who had been hung for committing a crime! A letter was published in the *Peterborough Standard* on the 11th day of March, 1899 from a gentleman "whose veracity may be relied upon": "Some time ago a man living in the north of the Isle of Ely was suffering from a disease of a cancerous nature. His suffering was intense and his face terribly swollen. He was discharged from Addenbrooke's hospital as nothing could be done for him. He appeared on the verge of sinking when a woman said 'I know what will cure you and it is this only. You must rub your face and neck with a dead woman's hand'. Soon afterwards the man heard that a woman had died in a village some distance away. He travelled to the house of death and implored the occupant to be allowed to stroke his own face with the dead woman's hand. The request was granted and he spent a long time in the operation. He quickly recovered and is now hearty and well".

The same paper also recorded that a Mrs. Brown, housekeeper to Messrs. Preston Brothers, Stowmarket, gives as fact that a friend of hers living at Norwich had a tumour of the eye, and hearing of this kind of treatment determined to apply it to her own case. It seems it worked too!

Miracle at Eldernell

The previous stories can be likened to miracles. According to a scribe attached to Thorney abbey it seems that a miracle did take place at the hamlet of Eldernell near Whittlesey. It happened when the Church was regarded with much suspicion and distrust and the overtures of the Dissolution were not far distant. Many miracles purported to have worked at monastic, cathedral and church shrines, turned out to be deceptive tricks devised by churchmen to defraud gullible people and overawe them into contributing to church coffers. However, there were some inexplicable "cures" which it would seem involved no trickery and may well deserve the title of miracle.

Robert Whyt of Whittlesey was a very sick man, so ill in fact it was considered by his friends and priests that he was close to death. One day in 1515 Robert received the last rites. He was quite unable to rise from his bed and had to be assisted to his feet by two friends. He appeared to be in some sort of trance but he recovered and declared that he had seen the Blessed Virgin and also Christ with bleeding wounds. He then divulged with great feeling to the astonished assembly matters of a religious nature.

Next morning the ill man got out of bed and made signs for a new linen shirt to replace his old garment. He then took his beads and a staff and proceeded to walk along the road to Eldernell, followed by an incredulous crowd. The morning was cold and frosty. Apparently he felt no pain for his efforts. Among those which travelled with him was the vicar of Whittlesey and when they arrived at Eldernell and had entered the chapel, Robert Whyt knelt down before the statue of the Virgin Mary and prayed earnestly. Then for a space of a quarter of an hour he could not speak, but then with great pain he opened his mouth saying "Lady help". The vicar and all present saw tears upon the face of the Blessed Virgin "as big as feches". The man who had petitioned for his restoration to health had his wish granted. The scribe of Thorney abbey testified to the event: "This is the truth, the curates of the same town with many other people will confirm it on a book" (the Bible).

The Vanished Chapel

Eldernell chapel was built in the early 15th century but fell into disrepair after the Dissolution of the abbeys. Eventually the chapel was totally demolished. An air of mystery attended the little chapel and it is odd that it was necessary to rededicate it in 1523. A licence granted to the Bishop of Down and Connor – the abbot of Thorney – dated July 20th 1523 instructed him to remove and inhibit such chalices, altar cloths, the superaltar and all ecclesiastical ornaments as *"had been abused, were old, deformed or improper"* and also to bless and reconsecrate others of the same sort. All this implies that some mischief had taken place within the chapel, that in some way it had been misused, so seriously it seems that the building was considered to be unfit for use until it had been reconsecrated. The will of John Wodford, chaplain and hermit of the Chapel of St. Mary of Heldirnal appears in the records of the Consistory Court of Ely. He left among other things a book "bochyre" and a missal for use in the chapel.

A Strange Whittlesey Will

One resident of Whittlesey left a very strange will. His sister was to receive £6,000 on the condition that she must carry out all his instructions to the last letter. Accordingly John Underwood's body dressed in every-day attire was placed in a green coffin, his head resting on Saradon's *"Horace"* , Bentley's edition forming his pillow and an edition of *"Milton"* lying at his feet. The right hand of the corpse clasped a small Greek Testament and a miniature edition of *"Horace"* was placed in his left hand. No bell was tolled and after the burial service had been read an arch was turned over the coffin and a piece of marble placed in the centre bearing the inscription *"Non omnis moriar 1733"*. The last stanza of the ode was sung by six mourners in which Horace deprecates any display of grief for

Gone are the shepherds of the Fens
Like rising ground from miry marsh around,
Where lambs and ewes leaped in fives and tens
Each sunny dawn upon the dew kissed ground.

the dead. This done, everyone sojourned to a house and partook of an excellent supper. As soon as the cloth was removed from the table the mourners performed a requiem in the form of another Horatical ode, then made merry with a cheerful glass and went home. Thus was fulfilled the testator's final injunction to "Think no more of John Underwood", and presumably his sister lived comfortably for the remainder of her earthly life.

Strange Journey

Still on the subject of man's transition from this world to that of the ethereal, there occurred at Wisbech soon after November 19th 1841, the start of a remarkable journey carried out in accordance with the wishes of Thomas Wressel, aged 63, who had died on that date. It was his wish to be buried at Clarborough, near Retford, where he had once lived. His sister dutifully had the coffin placed on a donkey cart and prepared to commence the 97-mile journey. The coffin which projected from the undersized cart had been covered with a ragged coverlet on which the deceased's sister sat. It took eleven days to complete this strange journey, the odd-looking vehicle with its sad burden reaching Clarborough on December 2nd. The body lay in the cart in an outhouse of one of the inns until the fourth day of the month when the curate at last committed it to the soil. The deceased man's 60-year-old sister paid the funeral expenses then returned to Wisbech with the donkey and cart.

Holbeach's Horrific Legend

A party that met frequently at the Chequers Hotel, Holbeach, for card games, agreed that should one of them die he, being a corpse, would have the final game with his friends. Eventually one of the party of four did die and was interred. One night his three colleagues went to the burial site, exhumed the body and prepared it for the game. Soon after, a man passing Holbeach church noticed a light in a window and, overcome with curiosity, obtained a ladder, put it against the window and looked in. A macabre sight greeted him. Sitting in the church were four people about to finish a card game, and one was heard to ask: "Dummy, can you one?" The dummy was the corpse of Jonathan Watson, a local doctor who had committed suicide by cutting through his veins and bleeding to death. It is said that in accordance with beliefs the body had been buried at the crossroads as it was considered inappropriate to perform Christian burials in cases of "felo de se". The three remaining gamists took the body and placed it in a chair near the communion table, put cards in its hand and, the corpse acting as a dummy, played its last rubber. The revolting affair had its origin in a drunken frolic and caused so much disgust in the town the participants were obliged to leave. To commemorate the sacriligious occasion a stanza was written by Eliza Cook, and is given in part:

> And they strode to the old church wall,
> Treading o'er skull and tomb,
> And dragged him out triumphantly
> In the murky gloom.
>
> They carried him down the chancel porch
> And through the fetted aisle;
> And many a heartless, fiendish laugh
> Is heard to ring the while.

It will be noted that according to Eliza Cook the churchyard was the place of burial. Some liberty must be ascribed to her, at least on the point where in her stanza she makes one of the gamesters drop dead when the church clock struck one!

The Plague at Ramsey

At Ramsey in 1666 a tailor took delivery of cloth from London and made a coat. Apparently the material was contaminated and the tailor's family all succumbed with the plague. On the morning of February 23rd, Major Cromwell for whom the coat had been made died of the plague and was interred next evening in the church. These initial deaths signalled a serious depletion in Ramsey's population, 400 residents being stricken. On July 16th Elizabeth Middleton died and was buried in her own garden, a not uncommon thing to do, restricted movement of a corpse thought to minimise the risk of infection.

Peterborough was frequently visited by pestilence and plague, parish records of the 17th century particularly notable in this field of study. Peterborough's most serious visitation was recorded in this manner: *"September 1665 – About this time the plague was supposed to be brought by a woman, a stranger from London who was entertained at the Woodgrounds in the 40 acres."* The first interment took place on September 22nd, 1665; the last in May 1667. During that period the number of deaths due to the plague amounted to 462. Fifty-seven died in June, 121 in July, 97 in August and 60 in September and 49 in October. Eleven people were buried in a single day. Most were interred in the grounds of the Pest House. Sometimes it was necessary to bury immediately as happened at Peterborough on at least 47 occasions. Registers state that burials took place "in his yard" and "in his close", "in an orchard" and "in their garden". The Pest House received 351 bodies but only 12 were buried in the churchyard. The vicar remained at his post throughout the visitation but a prebendary obtained licence to absence himself for fear of falling victim to the disease. The Fens got off relatively light, most travellers preferring to journey along the fringe areas rather than risk wallowing in the marsh! Undoubtedly this minimised risk of Fen people contacting the disease.

Cut off from the World

Parson Drove was one of those places which would wake up in the morning and find itself cut off from the world. There was an absence of good, hard roads and the parish was liberally intersected by numerous dykes and river banks which served to protect the roads such as they were and restrict water. The drainage system in the Fens being then none too reliable, dykes often overflowed and sometimes the protective banks were broken down by the weight of water. Each year the road from Parson Drove to Murrow became quite impassable, even for pack horses. On one occasion it took four horses as many hours to draw a wagon with a corpse from Sand Bank to Parson Drove for burial. The feoffees granted permission for it to cross their land in preference to the road, parts of which had disappeared beneath water. Permission was not easily obtained as opinion had it that the conveyance of a body across fields opened up a right-of-way.

Sometimes Fen floods were instigated by men who violently opposed the drainage scheme and they baulked at nothing in order to discourage the engineers. Many were the occasions when Fenmen ventured forth under cover of darkness to blow up wooden sluices, damage the banks and block the dykes. Notices sometimes appeared in local newspapers, as did the following in the Rutland and Stamford Mercury a few centuries ago: "Whereas some evil disposed person or persons did, during the month of April last, cut through the bank of the East Fen Catchwater drain, adjoining Halton road, whereby the flood waters caused great damage to the lowlands in the East Fen. Notice is hereby given that a reward of 10 guineas will be given to any person who shall give information of the offender or offenders to be paid on his or their conviction by the Treasurer of the Commissioners for Drainage by the River Witham". One wonders if the culprit was found and if so what was done to him.

River Nene, March c. 1900

Bevis

Rebellion at Coveney

Labourers working on the huge drainage scheme in the Ely area informed their supervisors that the people in the Coveney and Littleport districts were planning to rebel against them. A local dignitary who had observed small rebellions taking place wrote that if something was not done about it the Fen people would turn to general rioting. The poor in particular resorted to riots, arguing that their poverty arose from the fact that their livelihood was at stake due to diminished fisheries and "they did it for their future dinners". A Fenman, Edward Powell went to Ely and paid the town crier 2d. to proclaim that all that heard him should meet next morning at the Market Place and organise a petition to the King declaring the value of the wet fens before the drainage scheme was initiated. Fen men refused to help in the work and hundreds of foreigners were brought in to cut the drains and erect sluices.

Not only did civilians rebel against these things, military personnel at Ely rebelled for entirely different reasons. In 1809 part-time soldiers at Ely assembled for drill and training for the customary period of 28 days. They were told that they must pay for knapsacks and gaiters out of the guinea allowed to each man. The parade on June 19th was attended by an air of defiance. Several men called to their officers "No knapsacks!" and flatly refused to accapt them. The ring leaders were promptly arrested and four squadrons of German cavalry arrived from Bury St. Edmunds. The mutineers were addressed by General Auckland and a court martial followed. Each man received a severe whipping which prompted the remainder of the brigade to submit to similar humiliating punishment handed out by the German soldiers. The incident brought about a sharp reaction in English political circles.

A Flogging at Spalding . . .

The Spalding Guardian for February 27th, 1904 printed details from a correspondent then in his 78th year of an incident he remembered as a young lad. It apparently took place in 1836 on Spalding market place. The victim was a man who was said to have committed a serious offence. This person "had the reputation among other things of being a wizard and was brought into the town from the Pigeon, an ale house. He was secured to a farmer's cart drawn by a cart horse". The unfortunate man received his flogging as the cart moved steadily along a defined route and back to the starting point where he suffered more pain when salt was rubbed into his wounds for good measure. It was one of the last public floggings in England. Flogging of women was abolished in 1820.

. . . and at Wisbech

Two interesting buildings were demolished at Wisbech in 1810. They were the Shire Hall and the Shambles, bothing standing on the Market Place. The Shambles was a 16th structure of timber with a tiled roof. It consisted of a covered meat market with a large chamber above which served for most part as a granary and was supported by 16 pillars of Spanish chestnut. At the end of this building stood the Shire Hall. It was covered with a flat lead roof on which stood the town's pillory and stocks and also a cage in which felons were kept.

The more serious of lawbreakers – if they were spared being hung at Horseshoes Corner – were treated to a flogging in full view of the inhabitants. When the Shambles and Shire Hall had been demolished the pillory was placed in a cart usually drawn up in the Market Place near the old Robin Hood ale house. It is written that some wretches, locked head and wrists to the frame, bore their punishment with fortitude under the pain of being flogged while others "writhed and howled with each stroke". When the new Session House had been erected the floggings continued, victims being slowly drawn along High Street, around the Market Place and back to the Robin Hood. Processions were watched in grim contemplation by magistrates seated in the upper storey of the Butter Cross.

A man named Wilson, acting as the Mayor's Beadle, applied the strokes to bare backs. He was well known for his vehement manner and used his own system, plying three strokes in very rapid succession, then paused and repeated the process until justice was supposedly satisfied. On one occasion, thought to be the last, the poor victim, a person of poor physique, suffered dreadfully. His wounds turned to gangrene and he died.

Generations ago persons entering one of several timber yards adjacent to Wisbech port were not always there to purchase timber. The timber yard had a treadmill and lesser felons were taken there in the early 19th century to tread the mill and grind corn.

Prisoners-of-war were temporarily kept at Wisbech during the French Wars. The last "shipment" of these unfortunate soldiers sailed into the port in 1814. After peace had been proclaimed they left Wisbech in vessels with large numbers of compatriots who spent many years at Norman Cross Barracks, near Peterborough. The men were brought to Wisbech in lighters and then transferred to sea-going vessels. During their enforced stay at Wisbech the prisoners were allowed to communicate with local people through grated windows of cells. They sold ingenious models and toys which they produced from animal bones, human hair and straw. The soldiers from la belle France were highly talented country men and many of the beautiful and intricate items manufactured during their captivity are on display in Peterborough Museum and in the Wisbech and Fenland Museum.

Cow Dung used as Fuel

For centuries turf cut from the fen formed the principal fuel for use in cottages. Another custom in some parts of the flat land was the preparation of cow dung for similar purposes. It was converted into fuel by shaping the matter while still wet into the shape of turf, then drying it in the sun. Naturally, the processed dung gave out a repungant smell, whereas turf (which the writer once burned in an open hearth) yields not an unpleasant aroma. Both forms of fuel produced great heat and were slow burning.

Cock Fighting at Peterborough

Blood sport was, and in many parts of the world, still is the means of amassing large amounts of money. Cock fighting was frequently held at Peterborough and advertised locally in the manner here given: *"Cocking – To be fought for at the house of Mr. Peter Ellis, the Angel Inn, Peterborough on Tuesday, March 1st 1791. Subscription of 48 guineas, by 16 cocks, none to exceed 4lbs 8oz when fairly brought to the scales. All the cocks to be weighed and matched at 9 o'clock in the morning preceded by the first day's fighting; and to fight in fair reputed silver weapons (spurs). The owner of each cock to subscribe three guineas. The first eight winning cocks to have one guinea each; the next four 1 guinea each; the next two 1 guinea and the winning cock to have 34 guineas, giving to the last cock six guineas. The cock after the first round not to be drawn, but to fight nearest in weight together. Any cock weighing 4lbs 8½ozs to be excluded. The next day will be given a silver cup value £10 to be subject to the above weights and conditions. The winner to give two guineas to the second best cock. N.B.: A battle to be in the pit precisely at 10 o'clock each day"*. The following May, magistrates of the Soke made an order that it would be considered an offence were cock fighting to take place at any inn or public house in their division. These fights were attended by local gentry as well as men of the labouring class and the practice probably continued "underground".

Raced to Death at Wisbech

A race meeting was held in 1780 on a common near Wisbech. The purse was for £50 this contested by the owners of four five-year-old horses. It was the custom at this course to run the race three times with intervals of an hour. It was hard going for the beasts. One horse, Bellisimo, was driven so hard it fell down dead in the second heat and another, Daphne, died soon afterwards from similar pressure. G. Baretti, an Italian, attended the meeting and recorded

"At a stated time the horses with the jockies on their backs, start together and in a little more than the space of six minutes they run or rather fly three times round the circuit so that they run three miles in less than six minutes without being allowed an instant to breathe in."

What's in a Fen Name?

"Fen Tigers," "Fen Buzzards," "Fen Yellow Bellies" are a few name tags given to the Fenmen of old. Men using stilts in the marsh were dubbed "Cambridgeshire Camels." "Cambridgeshire Men" was a form of honour because they had fought the Danes and Normans when the rest ran away. Frogs were known as "Fen Nightingales" and in an adjoining county "Lincolnshire Bagpipes." From their amphibious habits Fenmen were referred to in the saying "Webfooted like a Fenman." His dowry was "Three geese and a pelt." "All hair and teeth like a Ramsey Man" was not at all complimentary, not was it intended to be with "As Bare as a Boston Scalp" or "As high as Boston Stump". A reflection of monastic opulence is seen with "All the carts that come to Crowland are shod with silver." "Arrested by the Bailey of Marshland" indicates a death through the Fen ague. "Lincolnshire where the boys drop soap and the cows drop fire" is interpreted as pig manure prepared and used as soap and cow dung dried and used as fuel. A spendthrift in the Huntingdonshire Fens was said to be "On his way to Beggar's Bush." "He was born at Little Witham" meant a Fenman was a fool (apologies to Witham). "As stunt as a burnt wong" and "As slough as a burnt wong" referred to leather thongs.

Discovery of an Abbot's Coffin

In February 1742, the sexton of Peterborough cathedral who was excavating a grave, discovered a large stone coffin containing the remains of one of the abbots of that former monastery. It lay in the south aisle of the Choir near the Queen of Scots monument.

The coffin lay on the ground and was partially covered by a pavement slab. It was noted that when the grave had been originally prepared care had been taken not to disturb the building's foundations. The abbot's body had perished and measured in length five feet two inches. It was covered with a velvet cope, figured and suitably bound. The pastoral staff, also bound, was four feet long, the crosier of gilt. Upon the least touch it fell to dust.

Next to the abbot's head was an earthen chalice and cover of thin pewter engraved with a rose. The shoe soles were sound and whole. The teeth by number and soundness indicated that the abbot had been a young man at the time of his death. Three abbots had been interred in that particular area: John of Chaux; Richard of London; and William of Woodford. Abbot Richard was a tall man who had died aged 82. The age of William of Woodford is not recorded but he was thought to be fairly old when he died as he had held a responsible post at the monastery earned through years of experience. The body was probably that of Abbot John, a Norman, who had become a monk at a very tender age and was distantly related to the then Queen. Brought to England he received his education at Winchester and there was appointed Prior. When he was still young he was appointed abbot of Peterborough and died in 1262 after serving in that capacity for 13 years. His death occurred at London and his body was embalmed and encased in lead. The flesh on his legs and thigh was still intact at the time of the coffin's discovery.

An account of Peterborough cathedral published on May 11th, 1833 tells of the discovery of a cope, the property of Abbot de Caleto "which was found when the church was newly paved, in a stone coffin. It is elegantly embroidered with sprigs, fleur-de-lys and gloriolae. In the centre is a Madonna and there is a border for the neck ornamented with figures of saints under double niches". The cloak had been nailed upon a white cloth just over the abbot's stone at the back of the altar. When exposed to air it disintegrated in many places and, according to the old verger, "was burned with other rubbish". Parts of the material were privately preserved.

Whirlwind Cakes at Leverington

The village of Leverington used to hold an annual feast, traditionally centred around "whirlwind cakes". Legend has it that a certain old lady of Leverington made some cakes to entertain her guests, but was visited by the devil who, creating a whirlwind, carried her off to the church steeple. The whirlwind cakes derived from the mischievous incident!

Old Shire Hall and Shambles: Wisbech Market Place; pulled down in 1816

T.A.Bevis

Mumping Day at Chatteris

Long ago it was the custom at Chatteris to hold a "Mumping Day." This involved men and women of all ages who went from house to house begging alms. The "mumpers" as they were called usually received a penny each. Some residents made a point of giving to widows and some only acknowledged widowers.

Bourne Custom

An old custom at Bourne, Lincolnshire known to be practised at the turn of the century, was alluded to in "The Daily Telegraph" of April 18th 1904. It followed these lines: an auctioneer took up position on the bridge in Eastgate. As each bid was indicated a boy started to run to a certain public house. The bid which was still unchallenged when the last boy returned was accepted as the rent of the field for the ensuing year and the bidder became the tenant. Then the company adjourned to take supper provided out of funds raised from the field, and two trustees appointed to dispose of the remainder of the rent by the distribution of bread.

The Straw Bear of Whittlesey

Years ago a strange custom was observed in Whittlesey involving a so-called straw bear. The custom has quite recently been revived. The "bear", a man covered in sheafs of straw is conducted around the town on the Thursday following Plough Monday. Apparently this ancient custom was for the confraternity of the plough to elect one of their number and dress him up as a bear with straw. He was then led through the town and clumsily and frantically entertained those who, on the previous day had subscribed to the rustics' meal of beef and beer and tobacco at which the said beer had presided. The custom was much enjoyed by sons of the soil as well as by the residents of Whittlesey, but more especially the children were well amused by the "animal's" amusing antics.

The Pancake Bell at Ramsey

There was revivied at Ramsey in 1889 the old custom of ringing the Pancake Bell. Ringing the bell on Shrove Tuesday originated as an act of summoning the people to church to be shriven – that they might be "in a state of grace and their penances and fasting during Lent the more acceptable to God." The proper time for ringing the pancake bell was at

15

11 a.m. but "with the aid of a knavish sexton" the bell was commonly sounded at 9 a.m., no doubt to the annoyance of some! The first pancake was given to the latest riser, a tradition which inspired someone to write this couplet:

Maids, fritters and pancakes enough see ye make,
Let slut have one pancake for companies sake.

Murder at Wisbech High Fen

The murder of William Marriot at Wisbech High Fen about two hundred years ago inspired not a little sympathy for the four men who were hung for the crime. It seems that the only witness of the assault was Mrs. Marriot, widow of the murdered man. Yet the lodger, William Clarke, who had risen from his bed and gone to the help of the woman and was himself attacked, was not even called to give evidence. At their trial the men involved had nothing to say except that the whole sordid business had arisen from a quarrel. Two of the accused declared that it was not the Marriots but one of the visitors who had gone outside to fetch a pail of water. On his return this helpful man found Marriot who seemed to be acting in a jealous rage, quarrelling with his wife and when the other visitor, an Irishman, expostulated, Marriot attacked a fourth man and hit him hard with the coal tongues, so hard in fact, they broke in half. At the same time Mrs. Marriot attacked the second man and seized him by the hair. Two of the men declared they had gone to bed when they saw Marriot and his wife arguing and had not been present when the fatal assault took place on July 3rd 1795. All four men, seized by panic, ran off and were apprehended three days later at Uttoxeter, Staffordshire. Twelve days later Marriot died. It took only a few minutes for the jury to return their verdict – that all four men were guilty of murder, when in fact only one answered the crime. In modern times it would probably be brought in as manslaughter.

The prisoners pleaded not guilty. They were accused of not only assaulting Mr. Marriot but also of attacking a lodger, then breaking open a box from which they removed a watch, several silver spoons, some cash and a coat most of which were found upon them in Staffordshire. The four were brought to justice by Mr. Egar and Mr. Letts of Guyhirn with the assistance of a constable. The Chief Justice presiding at Wisbech Assize passed sentence in the usual manner: "James Culley, Michael Quin, Thomas Quin and Thomas Markin. You have been tried by jury of your country and found guilty of the horrid crime of murder. A crime at which human nature revolts and which is punished by death in most countries of the world. All that remains of my meloncholy duty is to pass the dreadful sentence of the law upon you, which is: That you, James Culley, Michael Quin, Thomas Quin and Thomas Markin, be taken from hence to the place from whence you came, and from thence on Saturday next to the place of execution; and that you be there hanged by the neck till you are dead, and that your bodies be delivered to the surgeons to be dissected and anatomised, pursuant to the statute in that case made and provided. And may the Lord God Almighty have mercy on your souls."

A witness of the executions wrote: "The four unfortunate men who were born in Ireland had been several times employed as hired men by persons in the parish (Murrow) where the horrid crime was perpetrated. This morning, about eight o'clock they were conducted to the place of execution amidst an immense concourse of people, where they appeared to be very penitent, and after a short time spent in prayer they were launched into eternity." It was recorded that all four men "behaved with much serenity and composure, and with such an unusual resolution as greatly surprised many of the spectators. All four persisted to the last in the accounts they had given at the trial. In the great crowd there was almost a profound and devout silence."

After the usual time the bodies were taken down, two of them given to surgeons for dissection, the other two to be hung in chains. It is singular that these two, gibbeted as a warning to others, were they that had declared to the end that they had not been present when the fatal assault had taken place. The site of the permanent gibbet was about one mile west of Guyhirn on the north bank of Morton's Leam, an equal distance between the village and the actual scene of the murder.

The gibbeting resulted in degrading remarks against Irish people living and working in the area. They were unkindly greeted with unsavoury salutations, such as "Go to Guyhirn, Pat, and see your cousins hung" and "Corder for ye! Corder for ye! Returned the Irishman." (Corder murdered Maria Martin who was discovered some months later by her mother dreaming she was buried in the Red Barn at Polestead). By 1837 Guyhirn's gibbet post had completely decayed.

Circumstances surrounding this trial and executions give rise to doubt. Did a miscarriage of justice occur? The men's persistence to the very end of their lives in their accounts as to what had happened at the ill-fated house must at least have had some bearing during the trial where there was a reluctance to produce other witnesses. Why was not the lodger called? The men did not help themselves by stealing from the house and running away. Only one of them had remonstrated with the murdered man yet all were hung. It was nothing less than harsh justice, typical of the times when even to steal a crust of bread from a shop window could despatch one to kingdom come.

Fire at Ely Cathedral

In 1779 a carpenter walking by chance through the upper galleries of a transept at Ely cathedral discovered a fire blazing next to the famous wooden octagon tower. With assistance he tore up the burning boards and threw them onto the floor of the church. The conflagration began after a brazier had left a small fire unattended, a common fault in the old times, many a cathedral and abbey left roofless after an outbreak of fire.

A Whittlesey man's diary

The following notes are taken from a Mr. Lamb's diary. It is assumed that this gentlemen lived at Whittlesey and that events in the town and district were astutely observed by him.

1789 – 16 July: Mr. Thomas Ground's dyke drowned so deep that they carried the grass off to make it hay. He said he had had it for 50 years and never knew it before. William Batford's farm so wet that his crop was four inches deep; and nine inches fall at Green Sluice.

1795 – 3 Aug: Mr. Henry Madwell put his man John Brown in the Round House. (The man had been taken in custody). Abraham Bates let him have a pair of pickaxe and he got out. A very great mob carried him in a chair to his master's gate. The next morning his master had him taken to Wisbech and left him there. The mob broke Mr. Thorp's windows on 4 August. The next day a Court Leet was called to set on constables. They that had crops in King's Delph made an agreement with the parish to give £200 to be paid to the Poor Rate for the crop to stand 14 days after Lammas.

1797 – 28 Feb: The news arrived at Whittlesey that the Bank of England stopped payment and all other banks.

1797 – 4 March: Oats offered at Wisbech but no cash to pay for them, so a great many carried them home. If you went to the bank to get cash for £10 they would give you a five guinea bill and two guineas, and a note for the other to take next week.

1798 – 1 May: James Baker and Mr. Read, constables, went about the town to take names of all persons aged between 15 to 60. (In preparation for bolstering defences, it is assumed, France making a lot of threatening gestures at the time).

A few Fenny verses

PETERBOROUGH CATHEDRAL AND ST. JOHN'S CHURCH CLOCKS

When the Church and the Abbey, they both strike together,
There'll be either a death or a change in the weather.

And . . .

If in the Minster Close a hare
Should for itself have made a lair,
Be sure before the week is done,
A fire will rage within the town.

Should a hare in hasty flight
Scamper through the Ramsey Whyte,
Be sure before three days are gone,
A fire will blaze in Ramsey town.

Lutton Hill, Yaxley still mill and Whittlesey Mere,
Are the wonders of Huntingdonshire.

A wet Good Friday and Saturday
Brings plenty of grass but little hay.

Be ye early or be ye late,
I pray beware of Fleet Hargate.

Crowland as courteous as courteous may be,
Thorney the bane of many a good tree;
Ramsey the rich, and Peterborough the proud,
Sawtry by the way, that poor abbey gives
More alas, than all they.

Boston, Boston, Boston!
Thou hast naught to boast on,
But a grand sluice and a high steeple,
A proud conceited people,
And a coast where souls are lost on.

Though Boston be a proud town,
Skirbeck compass it all round.

The Fens have oftimes been by water drowned,
Science a remedy in water found:
The power of steam, she said, shall be employed,
And the destroyer by itself destroyed.

Gosberton church is very high,
Surfleet church is all awry,
Pinchbeck church is in a hole,
And Spalding church is big with foal.

Monday for health,
Tuesday for wealth,
Wednesday the best day of all.
Thursday for losses,
Friday for crosses,
Saturday no luck at all.

Kyme . . . God knows
Where no corn grows,
Nothing but a little hay:
And the winter comes
And takes it all away.

Huntingdonshire corn full good,
Lincolnshire men full of mighties.
Northamptonshire full of love
Beneath the gyrdle and nothing above.
Norfolk full of wiles,
Cambridgeshire full of pikes,
Holland full of great dykes.
The Lord that for us all did die,
Save all these shires.   Amen we say.

****

In Holland in the Fenny lands,
Be sure you mark where Croyland stands.
Croyland wine is but so-so,
Sedge instead of hay doth grow.
A bed like stone wherein to lie,
And so begone without goodbye.

A few Fenny verses (continued)

THE POWTE'S COMPLAINT

Come brethren of the water and let us all assemble,
To treat upon this matter which makes us quake and tremble;
For we shall rue it, if't be true that the Fens be undertaken,
And where we feed in fen and reed, they'll feed both beef and bacon.

They'll sow both beans and oats where never man yet thought it,
Where man did row in boats, 'ere undertakers bought it;
But, Ceres, thou behold us now, let wild oats be their venture,
Oh, let the hogs and miry bogs destroy where they do enter.

Away with boats and rudders, farewell both boats and skatches,
No need of one nor t'other, men now make better matches;
Stilt makers all and tanners shall complain of this disaster,
For they will make each muddy lake for Essex calves a pasture.

Wherefore let us intreat our ancient winter nurses
To show their power so great as t'help to drain their purses,
And send us good old Captain Flood to lead us out to battle,
Then Twopenny Jack with scales on's back will drive out all the cattle.

This noble Captain yet never was known to fail us,
But did the conquest get of all that did assail us;
His furious rage who could assuage? but to the world's great wonder
He bears down banks and breaks their cranks and whirlygigs assunder.

Great Neptune (god of seas) this work must needs provoke thee,
They mean thee to decrease, and with fen water choke thee;
But with thy mace do thou deface and quite confound this matter,
And send thy sand to make dry land, when they shall want
    fresh water.

(In support of the anti-drainage group, c. 1640.
Twopenny Jack is the Fenman's name for pike.
The whirligig was a windmill).

****

Sutton Long! Sutton Long! At every door a heap of dung
    Some two, some three . . .
    The dirtiest town you ever did see.

A few Fenny verses *(continued)*

Over singers, Swavesey ringers
Bluntisham runners, Earith gunners,
Colne noddles, Somersham suckeggs,
Fenton frogs, Pidley pancakes,
War boys, Wistow lads,
Bury creepheads, Ramsey scabs.

Rising was a seaport town
And Lynn it was awash;
But Lynn is now the
    seaport town,
And Rising fares the
    worst.

****

MARCH BRIDGE *(author unknown)*

The bridge at March across the Nene,
Erected long ago has been;
The stress although its pace is slow,
With force it onwards runs below
                    At March bridge.

The silent workers do the most
And not the noisy ones that boast;
The wise their tongues well bridl'd keep,
And like the Nene their thoughts are deep
                    At March bridge.

'Tis there they learn the latest news,
They freely talk and give their views
On all events throughout the day,
The gossipers have much to say
                    At March bridge.

The busy people hurry on,
In spite of spittle, smoke and fun;
A very strange and varied scene
The thoroughfare has always been
                    At March bridge.

The gangs meet there at early morn,
To start to hoe or cut the corn;
With merry laugh they haste away
To work with vigour all the day
                    At March bridge.

A few Fenny verses (continued)

The idlers gather there for fun,
Enquire for work, though wanting none;
They gaze while leaning o'er the sides
And watch the river as it glides
At March bridge.

There pass the newly-wedded pair,
Beginning life so gay and fair;
And funerals slowly move across,
The mourners grieving for their loss
At March bridge.

Thus one by one we hurry o'er
The bridge of time, to cross no more;
And like a stone dropped from a height
To waters deep, are lost to sight
At March bridge.

(c. 1900)

23

Bog Oaks thousands of years old

Bog oaks are sometimes discovered in the peat fen, particularly on land in Whittlesey and Littleport areas. Much theory relates to these interesting fossilised specimens, the common belief being that the trees were felled by immensely powerful gales two to three thousand years ago. Many of the trees, mainly rock-hard stumps, are left on the edges of fields after being struck by ploughs and brought to the surface. Celebrated antiquary, De La Pryme entertained a double hypothesis. Some trees, he wrote, have fibrous roots attached; others seem to have been cut or burnt down. Strangely still, he reasoned that some were squared and bored through. Even more strange, wedges of stone and iron were found in some and in one or two instances heads of axes came to light in the vicinty of the trees. What, then, can the answer be? Were the trees consisting of oak, fir and yew pushed over by gales, or perhaps an earthquake? Or were they purposely felled? One thing is clear, the trees contributed in some way to the formation of the turf. In their horizontal position they would obstruct any little streams which flowed near them, thus creating bogs. Many were unearthed in the 19th century and were seen to be so numerous in certain parts it can be truthfully said they had once formed a forest.

It has been surmised that the trees had been cut down by the Romans to deprive the British tribes of leafy shelter and materials to make fortresses from which the natives emerged to attack Roman stations. The destruction of these ancient trees refer to a very remote period and if tool marks on them and the presence of axes and wedges are anything to go by, we might well infer that the forests, or some at any rate, did not perish through some natural disaster. Several trees were discovered in an almost perfect condition. Some firs were thirty feet and oaks five-and-a-half feet long. Large quantities of hazelnuts and fir apples were also raised. As well as fossilised trees, the remains of unfortunate people were discovered, perhaps lost when attempting to cross watery fen. The fossilised trees are generally useless, but some were said to have been purchased by automobile manufacturers who used them for instrument panels. Some even found a use as pieces of furniture in Fenland homes.

Scandinavian longboat

At the time that the drainage scheme had finally achieved its aim about the middle of the 19th century, a number of interesting discoveries occurred in the shrinking fens. Agricultural workers in a field near Manea, discovered a couple of "posts" several feet apart. A month or

Fen marauder

Into the Fens the heathen with fury of Godless might,
No compassion, compelled by greed and lust sailed the night,
Striking fire upon the monasteries of watery waste,
Left as dead still forms bled by axe from life chaste.

Not another furrow!

two passed and it was seen that more timber had been exposed between the uprights, one of which was carved in the shape of a horses head. The men dug away the earth between the posts and realised they had excavated an ancient Scandinavian longboat which had become stuck or had sunk there at least a thousand years previously. Evidently the peat soil had had a remarkably good preservative effect upon the vessel which presumably had carried some proud warlord in his quest to pillage one or two local monasteries. The Fenmen that had discovered the boat, true to inbred tuition, did not report it, and according to one of them in later years, acting on the maxim "waste not, want not" they put the axe to the vessel for firewood and the Fens lost its claim to equal the famous longboat of Sutton Hoo! The carved head was saved and kept on private premises but no-one knows what eventually happened to it.

. . . and a Viking axe

Walking in his garden one day a century ago, a former Rector of St. Wendreda's church, March, heard his gardener chopping firewood. Going over to the man, the parson, a noted local antiquarian, was somewhat surprised to see him wielding a murderous-looking axe with which he made short work of a pile of tree branches nearby. The reverend gentleman was quick to recognise the instrument as none other than a Viking war axe. "Where did you get that axe?" he asked. "Why sir," replied the gardener, "It's like this: a few weeks ago I was doing some roding in a ditch and found it sticking out the soil. I takes it home and cleans it up, gave it a new edge and a handle and, believe you me, she chops like new!" Well, it made a change, no doubt, from cleaving skulls as in the case of a certain abbot at Crowland. This man had been informed of a Danish raiding party ransacking the island. The monks ran away but the abbot, putting faith before discretion, knelt before the high altar and prayed earnestly that the Danes would spare the community. He never knew what hit him. A Danish axe split his skull, then the marauders went away to try their luck at Thorney.

A bellringer, the writer remembers a visit with campanological friends to Crowland abbey to ring the bells, the first in the country to be broadcast on the airwaves. Near one of the bellropes, the longest in the world of bellringing, was a small wooden case with glass sides attached to the wall. Within it, staring balefully at the team, rested the cleft skull of Abbot Theodore shamefully purloined by a mischievous visitor in recent years. The Fens are full of surprises for antiquarians and archaeologists. Near Ely, Norman and Saxon weapons with chain mail came to light this century, lending support to what appears to be the truth of the epic siege of the Isle of Ely by William the Conqueror opposed by his renowned adversary Hereward the Wake. A scribe writing in the 12th century mentioned the discovery of weapons on the very same site.

Ancient weapons discovered in the Fens date from the Bronze Age to the 18th century. A farmer, grubbing an orchard at Murrow, turned up a very fine cavalry officer's sword of the Civil War. It was almost five feet from hilt to point. With it was an early type of hand grenade. Modern weapons were ceremoniously handed over to local authorities after the wars. Wisbech received a World War I battle tank and from the same period March was given a field gun which was sited near the river. Both were melted down to make weapons for World War II. On St. Mary's Green, Ely, a Crimean artillery piece guards the west front of Ely cathedral.

Dig deep to discover

Strange it is what one finds in the depths of the soil. In 1635 while deepening the river at Wisbech, workmen discovered eight feet below the river bed another river bed paved with stone! Along its course, at variously spaced intervals were seven boats which had been covered by silt for many centuries. When, in the same century, labourers raised stone slabs in the floor of the chancel of St Peter and St Paul church,

Wisbech, they discovered a boat a few feet below lying on what was apparently the bed of a primeval stream. In it were stones and hay which looked as if it had recently been mown. Everything was perfectly preserved. Men working at a depth of eight feet in moorland near Whittlesey found swathes of grass which gave the appearance of having been new mown. When making the foundations for Skirbeck sluice, near Boston, there was found sixteen feet beneath the surface a smith's forge and all the tools belonging to it including horseshoes. In driving piles for securing the foundations of a great sluice just north of Boston in 1764, at a depth of about eighteen feet beneath pasturage workmen came across tree roots just as they had grown as well as sea shells. When laying down a foundation sixteen feet deep at Magdalen, Norfolk, a stone eight feet long and a cart wheel were removed by workmen.

Near the River Welland at Spalding in 1696 labourers working at a depth of ten feet discovered a number of boats. In the vicinity of the same river at a similar depth old tap vats and a large quantity of horns and shoe soles with pointed toes turned up. Beneath the Fen, near March, lies a Roman road, originally about three feet thick and sixty feet wide extending from Denver in Norfolk to Peterborough, about 25 miles. It was constructed for military and commercial purposes by order, it is assumed, of the Emperor Severus, the first man to make a highway across the Fens. Several Roman artifacts have come to light in the vicinity of March. The remains of a Roman fortress and settlement lies on a small rise slightly north of the town boundary. Several Roman coins and a sizeable hoard of gold coins discovered in the 18th century were found at March, as well as a Roman skeleton. A few miles south east of the town are the remains of a Roman temple. Slightly north of March several human skeletons revealed by ploughing indicate a possible massacre in the dark and dangerous past. The site is near a junction of the old Roman road and another which led to the north. The unfortunate people could have been slaves, forced to make the road. It is well known that when slaves had expended their energies, the military put them to the sword rather than risk the possibility of them joining enemies.

Business for the Resurrectionists

Boats, coins, skeletons and cart wheels are only a few of the things yielded by Fenland soil. Entire human bodies, too, were illegally taken from it. A couple of centuries ago a new corpse was a valuable asset to a surgeon. The practice of taking bodies from their graves a day or two after burial was rife indeed and those involved in the practice made a tidy profit, too. It seems that certain hospitals and individuals allocated sizeable sums of money to ascertain the ready supply of bodies with no questions asked. The graveyard at St. Mary's church, Ely, had a notorious reputation for loss of bodies to that end and purpose. One can only assume that they headed in the direction of Cambridge, thirteen miles distant, to facilitate University medical research. One of the sextons at Ely seems to have been a man easy to manipulate. It appears that he passed information concerning funerals to people involved in the grisly business, and himself made the necessary arrangements for the "lifting" of suitable bodies. He turned a blind eye to any noise he may have heard at night when the Resurrectionists, usually three or four men, entered the churchyard and with care and stealth of cats proceeded to exhume the corpse. The sexton, albeit a rich man I wouldn't wonder, had an uneasy conscience towards the end of his earthly life. He confessed upon his death bed of his role in the sordid task and intimated that he had received as much as £10 for a nod and a nudge.

One of the problems in that foul business was that in the event of a person dying from cholera and typhoid for instance, which were common diseases a couple of centuries ago, removing a body so inflicted from the neutralising effect of soil, could well unleash disease upon living matter. In some cases bodies were buried in back gardens to minimise the risk of transmitting disease. All kinds of devices were tried in attempts to protect graves from interference. Concrete and granite slabs as well as heavy iron railing placed horizontally over graves being cemented into position immediately a burial had taken place. Some graves had little bells set on top of them, a cord descending through a tube, the end attached to the hand of the corpse. So terrified were some people of being buried alive! Only the wealthy could afford such precautions. The majority of burials represented the pauper class who took a chance – and often lost. Riots occurred in some towns, the public rightly incensed at the practice of body snatching. It was known for as many as five bodies to be found missing from a line of twenty graves. Yet it must be said thereby was built the foundation of the health and wellbeing of modern society.

Slept on a corpse

As revolting as all this was, a touch of amusement as well as the macabre attended the instance of an unfortunate fisherman who lived in the early nineteenth century at Yaxley near Peterborough. He had the reputation of being a habitual drunkard and it was his delight at the end of a busy day to do the rounds of public houses to such extent that his family never knew when to expect his return and was never alarmed at his absence at night. He had been known to sleep beneath a hedge or in a barn until his stupor had worn off. Apparently one night while attempt-

28

ing to walk home the man decided it was in his interest to sleep his cares away. He staggered into a field where stood a wooden shed. The door was unlocked and he entered in darkness and groped around, making out a pile of sacks in a corner. There, he decided, would be his bed and he prostrated himself and fell asleep.

When he awoke at sunrise he was racked with aches and pains from head to foot. His makeshift bed seemed to be filled with lumps and unusually hard. Curious to discover the cause of his discomfort he pulled away empty sacks and found one which was tied at both ends. Untying one end the fisherman made an horrific discovery of a corpse of a young woman, stiff with rigor mortis. It turned out that the woman and died a few days previously at the age of 24 years and that her name was Elizabeth Fry. All stupor swept aside the man fled from the scene and was observed by a horseman travelling along the road towards the field. He stopped the fisherman and asked him why the hurry. The shocked drunkard, having regained his wind, told the mounted man of his gruesome discovery. Listening with pretended surprise the rider invited the fisherman to join him for a glass of wine at an eminent surgeon's house. Our Yaxley friend thanked him and wisely declined the invitation then hurried home. In due course the matter was reported.

At the Coroner's inquest evidence revealed that the woman, who had been buried at the cemetery near St. John's church, Peterborough, had been "snatched" that night by the local group of Resurrectionists and taken to the shed in the field owned by the surgeon. He, the only surgeon in the city, practised at the Infirmary and there can be no doubt that he and others of his profession at that time, kept contacts with individuals "in the know" and paid handsomely for fresh bodies dissected to promote medical knowledge. The surgeon was a distinguished member of the community and much valued for his work. It was not surprising therefore that the matter was conveniently dropped and the surgeon reinstated. However, it was noted that the gentleman on horseback, known as "Squire" and, as it turned out, leader of the "snatchers," had hastily left the area and was never seen again. As for the fisherman: well, we may imagine he drank modestly after all that.

The Chatteris elephant

Not a few interesting discoveries were made at Chatteris. In the early years of the 19th century, part of the skeleton of an elephant was brought to the surface from a hole ten feet deep. It was generally thought that the animal had belonged to a circus visiting the town. In 1824 an earthen vessel was dug from the ground, containing a thousand copper coins of Roman origin. A double-edged sword, the hilt lavishly adorned with figures of fighting men, in a remarkable state of preservation, was also discovered at Chatteris. In 1757 a tumulus was opened near the Ferry Turnpike two miles from the town. In it were several human skeletons, as well as a spear, the umbo of a shield, an urn, a glass vase and several other items predating the Roman conquest.

Pretty gardens and "ugly" people

For centuries the River Nene at March was a centre of gossip and industry. It was written that it looked very pretty two hundred years ago – and still does – riverside residents tending flower gardens and vegetable plots with infinite care. Then, the river was not quite as deep set within its banks as it is nowadays, but it teemed with commercial activity. As early as the reign of Elizabeth I March was noted as a minor port with eight boats and did considerable business in timber, coals and corn. Barges turned up with odd loads, too! Such as redundant stones and timber from the ruination of Thorney abbey for use in the restoration of cottages on the riverside. Floorstones and rubble were cheaply purchased for repairs to St Wendreda's church, these items brought from Thorney by a townsman assisted by a boy with a horse drawn tumbril. There are several old cottages, some 17th century and possibly older, along March waterside with interesting ceiling beams. Some beams may have had a use in former ecclesiastical buildings. The Ship Inn, along Nene Parade, boasts a good display. It is one of the oldest pubs in March and once had a lock-up where drunks spent a night of stupor. A flour mill once kept The Ship company and barges loaded and unloaded materials from a small wharf adjoining a tunnel in the river bank and beneath the road, terminating in the basement of the mill at the rear of the pub. This old hostelry and the White Horse, while not forgetting The Acre were favourite meeting places of Fen bargemen. The White Horse attractively sited along West End has seen a few centuries pass by in this lovely old part of March with bushes and trees and very pretty gardens. A 17th century house nearby contains massive beams which the writer thinks are far too large for a normal house and, in his opinions may have been purchased (or purloined!) secondhand.

In 1785 a flotilla of twelve barges passed along the river en route to Whittlesey Mere. It was commanded by the "Admiral of the Fleet" who, with a number of well known gentlemen, were navigating the Nene to their destination where they had arranged a few drinking and smoking parties with sumptuous meals of Fen bred fish and eels, wild fowl and porkers. The vessels were crammed to the roofs with victuals. The fleet entered Ugg Mere and Ramsey Mere. The "Admiral" kept a diary of day-to-day events and keenly observed the state of the Fens and the rivers, the gardens and above all the inhabitants of the places they passed through. Of March he wrote partly in unsalutory terms, "The gardens are pretty," then to his uncharitable way of thinking, "but the women of the town are ugly." Fen women of the 17th and 18th centuries had the reputation of lacking feminity, this attributed to the very rigorous life they lived, many of them being bread winners and more adaptable to working in the fields than in kitchens.

The feast at Whittlesey Mere

Without doubt the "Admiral" enjoyed his party on the waters of Whittlesey Mere. It had long been the custom of the gentry to meet there and enjoy themselves. In 1669 one such occasion was recorded in a poem of ninety-nine hexametres, and it took place on a large, flat-bottomed boat near Frog's Hall. A number of distinguished clergymen were present. According to a witness the feast began with melons served with sugar and pepper and salt. Port wine was served. Then followed venison, pastry, rounds of beef, chicken breasts and legs and shoulders of mutton. The hunting of deer and bringing the ox to the party were grandly described in verse. But that was not all! Poultry, pullets with bacon, salted tongues and more wine followed. Finally roast apples were brought to the regaled guests, rounded off by tarts, cakes swilled down with more wine and cider for good measure. After all that, the host took out a tinder box and set fire to rotten wood, filled his pipe with tobacco from a silver box and settled back in a most contented manner, as no doubt did the rest. Those old-time Fenmen knew how to feast!

Wisbech cobblers on strike

One must eat and in order to eat one must have sufficient money. In 1539 the cobblers of Wisbech, twenty-two in all, finding times hard, met to air their views at a place called Mill Hill just beyond the town. It was agreed that they ask 1s. 3d. for every dozen shoes sewn or they would refuse to work. One, a servant of Robert Smyth swore upon the bible that he would not stitch a dozen shoes under that amount. The cobblers were apprehended by constables but the magistrates thought fit to let the matter drop and shoes continued to be stitched at the old rate!

Retired
Fennies

Ring's End and "The Ring"

The hamlet of Ring's End stands close to the site of a medieval building known as Tower House. This was built in about 1470 at the junction of Morton's Leam and the River Nene to survey the progress of the Leam from Guyhirn to Stanground. "The Ring" from which Ring's End derived its name is described as land "within a bank beginning at Keeke's Mill and thence to Tower House and thence to Hobb's House (on the bank of the Sixteen Foot river) and so to Tilney Hurne and thence by Maries dam and so by Elme Leam to Friday Bridge and thence by Redmore Dyke and Begdale and so by Gold Dyke to Keeke's Mill again." This extensive bank roughly formed a circle, or "ring."

New "Laundry" at Ramsey Abbey

In 1288 the convent at Ramsey abbey desired to build a new laundry (lavatorium) of good and durable metal, thirty-three feet in length and two-and-a-half feet or more in height, together with copper keys (clavibus) of subtle design and richly gilt. Workmen engaged on the project were to receive two loaves of bread, one of monks bread, also two gallons of beer from the convent cask, and on flesh days a dish of meat and a pittance. For each of the servants every day two loaves of the hall and two gallons of household beer. On fish days (no meat to be eaten) a dish of fish. It was not actually a laundry being built but a lavatory and was likely constructed in the cloister. Many examples of "lavatoriums" remain built of stone like the one at Peterborough cathedral, but it is thought that not a single metal one remains.

A heathen place

Samuel Pepys, the famous diaryist, visiting relatives at Parson Drove, a village he did not much care for, described it in his diary dated September 18th 1663, as "a heathen place." He wrote, "I began a journey through the Fens along dykes where sometimes we were ready to have our horses sunk to the belly; we got by night with hard riding to Parson Drove - a heathen place - and found my cousins in a sad, thatched cottage. To bed up, and after eating a dish of cold cream which was my supper last night, too, away over sad fens, all the way observing the sad life which the people of the place who they do call breedlings if they be born there, do live." One supposes his journey took him through Guyhirn, "the corner of the saltwater ditch," another sad place in his time, with a gibbet on which was hung the bodies of felons after execution at Wisbech.

March duck takes off

The tapering spire of St. Wendreda's church, March, carried a fine copper weathervane shaped like a duck. One night long ago, aided by a fierce gale, it decided to fly for real. It spiralled into the sky and landed in the garden of a nearby house, where it was promptly impounded by the owner who refused to hand it over to the churchwardens, saying that as it came down in his garden he regarded it as his property on the doubtful basis of "finders keepers." The spire was inspected and was found to be cracked in the upper section, which necessitated being rebuilt. An old photograph exists showing three steeplejacks balancing themselves on a plank across the tip of the spire about one-hundred-and-forty feet above the ground; the centre man, actually the foreman, is seen standing without support on the spire! A new arrow-shaped weathervane was set upon a spherical container in which, it is said, was placed bric-a-brac reminiscent of the Victorian age, including a local newspaper, The Cambridgeshire Times and coins.

Peterborough strong man

Steeplejacks need to be strong. Certainly they must have s strong head for heights. In 1749 Thomas Topham of Peterborough demonstrated remarkable displays of his not inconsiderable strength, like that of twisting an iron poker two and a quarter inches in diameter around his neck and bending one three inches round on his arm. He could lift a table six feet long with his teeth, a half-hundredweight hanging from the opposite end! Topham would lay his head upon a chair and his feet upon another and suffer four men to stand upon his stomach and while in that position by the motion of his body heave the "passengers" up and down. With his fingers he would roll up a pewter dish seven pounds in weight as though it were paper. Another favourite partypiece was that of breaking a rope that was capable of bearing the draught of a fully developed horse. For these exhibitions he charged each spectator a shilling.

The siege of Crowland

During May 1643 information came from Crowland that Captain Welbie, described as a pernicious and desperate malignant against King and Parliament, and a mischievour mover of rebellion in this part of the Fens, had "persuaded" the inhabitants of Crowland to obey him and with him and other commanders declare themselves against Parliament, and fortify the town with trenches and other obstructive defences.

When this was done, Captain Welbie and his soldiers approached Spalding, a town bereft of armed men, and beset the house of a Mr. Ram, a minister, whom they took captive and also John Harrington with two others, a Mr. Horn and Mr. Slater, both sixty years of age. The reason given for seizing these peaceful men was that the minister had supposedly written a letter to the inhabitants of Crowland appealing to them not to oppose Parliament. Crowland had two clergymen who were known to have orchestrated objections against the appeal and who supported Captain Welbie. The Spalding men were taken to Crowland and imprisoned and denied opportunity to pray.

This state of affairs continued for three weeks during which the prisoners were subjected to much abuse. Meanwhile the citizens of Spalding got themselves together and with arms and some regular soldiers marched against Crowland. At eight o'clock on the first night the opposing forces faced each other and the prisoners were carried down the bulwark on the north side of the town and kept there all night among rude and coarse soldiers. The Spalding contingent could not advance for fear of their captive friends receiving injury or worse. The following night the prisoners were taken to an alehouse and cast into prison again next day. Seeing their four friends taken away from the bulwarks, the Spalding men advanced but the prisoners were again brought out and placed before the oncoming army as cannons hurled missiles over their heads. Before the assault a Spalding drummer was sent to peaceably summon the town but the man was wounded and he, too, was taken prisoner.

All the prisoners were set upon the breastworks and made to stand there for three hours, their friends from Spalding unaware of their presence, actually shooting towards them but happily missing. Captain Harrington of Spalding took a musket from a soldier, charged it with powder and shot three times at his own father without knowing who it was. Other Spalding soldiers also opened fire at the prisoners standing calmly upon the fortifications. When they realised what was happening the Spalding men aimed their muskets well to the right of the hostages, but the Crowland garrison instantly moved the hapless men into the line of fire. Little could be done on that side of the town that day, the fortifications well lined with soldiers backed by Crowland civilians armed to the teeth with hassock-knives (long scythes) and other weapons.

The fury of the fight abated but increased in another direction, where Mr. Ram and Mr. Horn had been placed in range of shot. By this the besiegers supposed Mr. Ram was none other than the Rev. Styles of Crowland for whom they had little respect. The Spalding force steadily advanced within musket range and opened fire at the prisoners and others in the vicinity. Miraculously the men escaped the fusilade and some shots went past their ears, pieces of lead falling half a musket length short of the prisoners.

The men continued to suffer in this way for three hours or so, and the Spalding force realising who they were started to withdraw. The two prisoners were then released and removed to the prison together with three others including the wounded drummer who had been subjected to similar treatment on the west side of Crowland. The besieging forces on the north side, seeing the way clear, began to attack on a heavy scale and instantly the defenders set up the prisoners again and the attack failed. The Crowland garrison took this as a victory and then made a fatal error. One man, a priest named Jackson, later had the prisoners brought from their cells and by way of a form of thanksgiving for the "victory" read aloud certain Collects. Inspired by this little ceremony, the garrison troops spent the rest of the day drinking, revelling and mocking the Parliamentary forces surrounding the town.

The besiegers, taking advantage of their opponents' preoccupation, formed themselves into three assault groups and stormed Crowland from different directions, climbing the bulwarks and entering the streets before the defenders could realise what was happening. The assault forces were respectively commanded by Col. Sir Miles Hobert, Col. Sir Anthonie Irbie, and none other than Col. Oliver Cromwell who had come to their assistance. Crowland fell but not before the prisoners were brought from their cells for the umpteenth time and pinioned to stakes in the wet ground and fallen into the mud where they lay before being set free by their victorious friends.

The rebel commanders left their men to their fate and escaped. Several Crowland inhabitants who had helped the rebels were seized and taken into custody at Colchester, Ipswich and various other places. The general Commander of the Parliamentary force was Col. Edward King of Ashby on Lincoln Heath, a highly capable officer and High Sheriff of Lincolnshire.

Crowland abbey is said to have been severely damaged in the bombardment by Parliamentarian artillery, understandably so as the church was used by the defenders. The original description of the battle makes no mention of the abbey, but their is little doubt that its position and especially the tower would prove very useful as a lookout for the town's defensive positions. During the Civil War many churches and large mansions in the land were requisitioned by both sides and as a result damaged. Crowland was the gateway to the Isle of Ely which was essential to the Parliamentary cause, fortresses being set up at Wisbech and March for the security of the western flank of the Eastern Counties Association.

Doddington Yeomen Cavalry

A tablet in St. Wendreda's church, March, was placed there on May 29th 1828 to commemorate the Doddington Yeomen Cavalry, first formed on May 2nd, 1798 to serve as Horseguard in the event of the French invading England. Local Yeoman units, older versions of the Home Guard of the Second World War, were common during the French Wars and they disbanded when threat of invasion had receded. Doddington troop continued in service for thirty years and was released from duty by King George the Fourth. The officers were allowed to retain their commissions and the Yeoman Cavalry pennant occupied an honoured place in the church until about 1950.

Distribution problems

In about 1918 an "extraordinary outrage" occurred at Coveney, near Ely. For four days the poor folk of the village deliberated among themselves the supposedly inappropriate manner of the distribution of alms. People went into the streets making incitive proclamations to the effect that they would meet at the church gate on Easter Monday and take possession from the feoffees the charity lands from which they derived benefit and divide them between themselves. The matter was duly reported by the constable and the magistrates at Ely issued a warrant for the arrest of the nine ringleaders. They were taken to Ely in a covered waggon, were tried and found guilty and presumably served time in the city gaol, a place quite notorious for certain cruel devices designed to create as much discomfort as possible for the unfortunate victims.

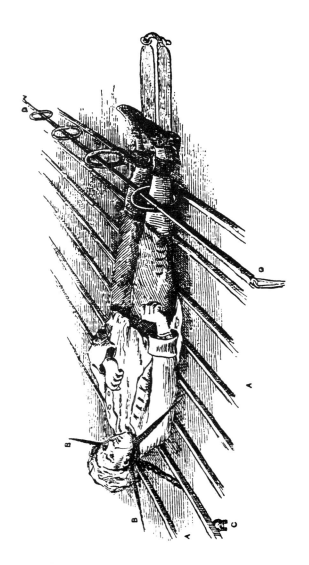

TORTURE AT ELY PRISON

This picture which was printed in Fenland Notes and Queries in 1906, illustrates the type of torture inflicted upon prisoners at Ely in the middle of the eighteenth century. The object of this barbarous practice was to prevent the victim from changing his posture and to prevent rest. The iron rods caused injuries to the legs, back and neck.

Theft of a March horse

"The London Gazette" published for Monday, January 10th to Thursday, January 13th 1686, contained the following notice: "Taken out of the Griffin Inn stable the first instance in the town of March in the Isle of Ely, a brown gelding bobtail'd about nine years old, thirteen hands and a half high, something low backed, a small star in his forehead, a little yellow about the eyes, a brown nose, with a crack overthwart his hoof before, supposed to be taken by a tall, lusty man with fair hair, full eyes, about twenty-four to twenty-five years of age. Whoever gives notice either of the man or horse to Mr. Samuel Keeble at the Griffin Inn aforesaid, or to Mr. Thomas Urdall at the Swan-With-Two-Necks in Turtle Street, Westminster, shall have a guinea." One wonders if the culprit was caught. If he was, it's a certainty that the gallows at Tyburn, or that at Wisbech, witnessed his hesitant approach!

The Prodigal Son of March

Another purloined horse featured in the exploits of Robert Wilson, native of March, and hardly an eminent citizen of the town. He took his father's horse without permission and rode away into the world. This act led him to an unusual life of adventure and he later wrote a book about it, subscribed by a number of March citizens. In it Mr. Wilson was described as a famous pedestrian, and all things considered he deserved that honourable title. He must have been well familiar with horses as he rode them through the late years of the nineteenth century in most countries of the world. He walked a great deal as well. So much so he was truly an accomplished pedestrian and famous if foolhardy, taking numerous risks and his life threatened many times. Wilson was caught up in mutinies and civil strife and he took part, sometimes unwillingly, in numerous hair-raising escapades. He was accused by foreign powers of spying and seemed to have a charmed life among hungry headhunters! He was imprisoned and set free – sometimes to his disadvantage it being often desirable to be locked up in a cell out of harm's way. Foreign agents suspected him and he was forced to move on. It was a rare adventure but, at last, March's prodigal son decided that enough was enough and longed to return to his Fenland home to seek his father's forgiveness. After several weeks of travel he stood upon the edge of the Fens and journeying on espied the old church spire welcoming him home. Then, cruel fate. Entering the family house he learned that his father had died a few weeks previously. Encouraged by friends he commenced writing his book in which he declares that no-one living had travelled as extensively in the world as he.

Arguably the finest late mediaeval tower in Great Britain, Boston Stump, as it is affectionately known, accommodates twenty-five bells, ten ringable in the traditional manner. They were recast and augmented between the two Great World Wars by benevolent Americans to commemorate the historic links between Boston, Massachusetts and Boston, Lincolnshire. The Pilgrim Fathers sailed from the latter port and in 1631 in America built a new town on an earlier settlement which was called Tremont and renamed it Boston.

Fenland earthquake

The following particulars are taken from the notes of Maurice Johnson, founder in the 18th century of the Gentlemen's Society of Spalding, with additions by William Smith: "As early as February in this year (1750) preliminary shocks were felt in different parts of England and, except June, not a month passed without some record of an earthquake somewhere in the country. One was felt severely at Spalding and the neighbourhood . . . For a fortnight before, the weather had been serene, mild and calm, and one evening there was a deep, red aurora australis covering the cope of heaven, very terrible to behold . . . It (the earthquake) lasted only a few seconds, but during that time houses tottered and heaved up and down; a rushing noise accompanied the shock, slates and tiles falling from the rooftops of homes; pewter and glasses fell from the shelves; windows were generally rattled and sometimes broken. Other places experiencing the shock included all Holland (South Lincolnshire), Peterborough and Wisbech. Then it passed over the whole breadth of Ely Fen and reached Bury in Suffolk." The centre of this earthquake was thought to be in Deeping Fen.

Another earthquake happened soon the first and affected several places including Crowland Fen, Thorney Fen, Whittlesey Fen, the whole of the Bedford Level and all of Ely Fen. Mr. Johnson wrote that it caused a channel at Spalding to fill with silt and it had to be cleansed and deepened. Several houses suffered serious cracks to walls and foundations. (Note – A minor earthquake was felt in the north-west Fens early in 1992. It is thought that its centre was slightly west of Peterborough and the shock was felt as far as Wisbech and March).

The tower of Boston's great church

Matthew Humberstone, historian, wrote this note from a mediaeval manuscript in 1699: "Anno 1309 in the third year of Edward ye Second. On Monday after Palm Sunday in ye same year, the miners began to break ground for ye foundation of Boston Steeple, continuing till midsummer following at which time they were deeper than the haven by five feet, and there they found a bed of stone upon a spring of sand; and that lay upon a bed of clay. Upon the Monday next after the Feast of St. John Baptist was laid the first stone by Dame Marjery Tilney, upon which she laid 5l. Sir John Fruesdall (priest) gave also 5l. and Richard Stevenson, a merchant gave 5l. more and these were all the gifts given at that time. The altitude of the steeple and length of the church are equal, viz: each 94 yards. The steps of ye steeple are 365, windows 52, pillars 12, as equal to the daies, weekes and months in ye yeare."

Blubberhouse Corner

This was a sharp and very awkward bend in the River Ouse above Magdalen Bridge, once a rickety collection of rotten piles and projecting iron bolts, very dangerous to navigators. Below this bridge, near Wiggenhall St. Peter's, there is a place where the river almost dried at low water spring tides. There one would see a number of young inhabitants grubbing in the water up to their knees, picking up what was known as "coals," more likely the remains of an ancient forest. The stuff was quite black and parts of fossilised trees. "Blubberhouse" survives from the time when there was a whaling fleet at King's Lynn and it is supposed that the process of extracting oil from whales took place on a bend in the river. In the 19th century a great many whales' jawbones existed in Norfolk parishes. There was at Lynn an old house bearing the date 1605 on a bracket from which hung a sign showing a harpooned whale flinging boats in all directions. The entrance of a driveway at March has remains of a couple of such jawbones. These are said to have been given in the 1850's by a sea captain who, it is thought, was buried in St. Wendreda's churchyard. His headstone showed a sailing ship sinking in a turbulent sea.

Tide-out

Moans of a "Flying Eight" Lass

Sozzled again!

"What you doing down there missus?" asked the dutiful constable.

"If yer wants to know, I've a-sozzled meself, and so would you if you had been a-picking taters aginst the old Fen blow which gits up yer nose, in yer ears and in yer knickers. Arter all that yer gits on yer bike with t'others and pushes all the way to Manea. And what do yer know, that old husband a mine is playing domies with his useless mates and is so teetered with drink he can't even put the brussels on. Well, two can play that game."

(The "Flying Eight" were teams of eight country women riding cycles, travelling miles in all weather to work in fields, picking potatoes and hoeing beet).

Thirteenth century diary

Matthew Paris, noted thirteenth century historian, made several references to the Fens in his Chronica Majora. A few are reproduced here:

870 – Destruction of the monasteries of Crowland, Thorney, Ramsey, Ely and Hamstede (Peterborough).

1071 – The Earls Edwin, Morcar and Siward with Egelwin, Bishop of Durham, associate themselves with many disaffected persons and rebel against William the First. They take themselves to the forests and waste places; then they do what mischief they can to the King's property in various places and finally seek refuge in the Isle of Ely. There, under the leadership of Hereward they make frequent sallies and do much damage. A wooden fortress is constructed which is called to this day (c. 1225) Hereward's Castle. The king comes against them, surrounds the Isle with his forces, makes roads and bridges, renders the deep swamps passable for men and beast and builds the castle at Wisbech. (Read "Hereward: The Involvement of the Monasteries of Ely and Peterborough": Trevor Bevis).

1165 – January 27th: Earthquake in the Isle of Ely, Norfolk and Suffolk which knocked men down and caused church bells to ring.

1216 – The Isle of Ely laid waste by Walter Buc and the Brabacons, and by the Earl of Salisbury. Thrice they came over from Stuntney. With drawn swords they entered the cathedral and the Prior only saved the place from being burnt by a payment of 209 marks. Much cruelty and extortion was practiced.

1216 – King John, after ravaging Norfolk and Suffolk, goes to Peterborough, Crowland and Lynn. He loses his baggage in the Wash; is later ill at Swineshead but goes on to Sleaford and Newark, where he dies on October 18th. He is buried at Worcester. *(Note* – The King is said to have lodged at Wisbech Castle before recommencing his fateful journey across the Ouse tributary somewhere between Walsoken and Walpole St. Andrew).

1236 – Most disastrous inundations on the morrow of St. Martins (November 8th). Anchors were torn from vessels in port. Multitudes of men, sheep and oxen were drowned, trees torn up by the roots and houses overthrown. By the seaside bodies were tossed about on the coast, and especially was this the case near Wisbech, so that in one single day in a neighbouring town of no great population as many as a hundred bodies were buried.

1254 – Great sterility in autumn through inundation of sea. Crops by the sea were all rendered worthless by the salt. This eruption of the sea had been foretold the previous winter. As an example of the loss of the harvest it is stated that the Prior of Spalding from all his lands near the coast, could not get a single handful of grain.

1256 – A dispute of long standing between the Bishop of Ely and the Abbot of Ramsey with regard to respective boundaries came to an amicable conclusion. Formerly the Fens were inaccessible. There were no dwellings, no foothold for man or beast, only sedge, deep beds of mud, marshy thickets of reeds, the homes of birds not to mention demons. Now all is converted into delightful meadow land and arable ground.

Have straw . . . will work

Several years ago workless labourers and others wishing to change their jobs, gathered near the old bridge at Wisbech on certain market days. They wore straw in their hats, signifying they were for hire. A prospective employer approached a man and after a few preliminaries invited him to a nearby inn. A coin was placed in the hired man's hand and a drink offered. A binding contract thus was made. The cattle market at Wisbech was a colourful, if smelly, venue, a motley assembly of shrewd Fen folk weighing on the auctioneer's every word. Old timers enjoyed baccy sessions and idle gossip in the taverns, downing prodigious amounts of ale at 2d. a pint!

Yellow Belly alias the Breedling

Anciently, true Fenmen and women were known by upland people as Breedlings. The damp environment probably had some effect on the skin colour of Fen dwellers as it is said that they were a greyish yellow – not a good, healthy looking colour although they generally lived to a ripe old age. Hence the Breedling was given a second title, that of Yellow Belly. That was because he was supposed to have looked a bit like eels taken from the black fen water. It is an old title for a Fen person. In 1537 the last abbot of Crowland, attempting to curry favour of Thomas Cromwell, devourer of monasteries, sent him a barrel of pickled eels, each a fine specimen of its watery habitat, with a sleek underpart of yellow and blue-grey. One supposes it to be appropriate for a Fen person to be thus called, the eel none other than the lord of the meres and with sticklebacks the prime breeder of these parts. Why shouldn't the people be named after his opalescent belly. And what is more, the people too, were good breeders.

Meres were the Fens' self-stocked pantries. A bill of fare from Ramsey, dated 1566, states that the mere in that area provided pickerells, roches, tench, pike, green pickerells, spawns, knobbers, bream, hard-bird, shallowes and, of course, eels in their thousands. Possibly the eels were overshadowed by the wiry little stickleback. This miniature fish bred in such abundant quantities shoals of them were literally shovelled from the ditches and used as manure on the fields. Reed and sedge were useful materials for wildlife as well as men, but Fen grass had no such reputation.

> *"Her grass so blady is and harsh,*
> *It cuts the cattle's mouth;*
> *In her ditches bred are fish of muddy taste,*
> *Than feed on them the crows would rather starve."*

Duck and mallard excelled on the meres and decoys. One old man declared that he had seen the pond of his decoy "so full of fowl that it looked as if you could not prick a pin in anywhere." Fen-Bill Hall knew the 18th century Fens like the back of his hand. He once said that a decoy pond a mile away from his home was so full of food that "it was apparently impossible for an egg to drop withour lifting one." At evening when the birds quitted a pond to feed, it was said to have "risen." Once raised out of the water, wildfowl noisily made their way to the feeding places and "the spacious air was darkened with their flights." In Fen-Bill Hall's eyes they flew in multitudes above his house "that a stranger would suppose it to be distant thunder."

In praise of the Fens

An extract from Hissey's *Over Fen and Wold,* published in 1898:
"A strange, weird world the English Fenland seems to unfamiliar eyes, especially when seen under a brooding sky; and there is a peculiar quality of mystery that baffled description and cannot be analysed in the deep blue-grey palpitating gloom that gathers over the Fenland distances when they lie under the threatening shadow of some coming storm. Under such conditions the scenery of the Fens is pronouncedly striking, but even under ordinary circumstances a man can have but little poetry in his soul who cannot admire its wild beauties, its vast breadths of luxuriant greenery over which the eye can range unrestricted for leagues upon leagues on every side, its space expressing distances and its mighty cloud-scapes, for the sky-scape is a feature in the Fenland prospect not to be overlooked; in fact I am inclined to think that its sky scenery – if I may be allowed the term – is the finest and most wonderful in the world. It is worth a long journey to the district if only to behold one of its glorious sunsets, when you look upon a moist atmosphere saturated with colour so that it becomes opalescent, and the sinking sun seen through the vibrating air is magnified to twice its real size as it sets in a world of melting rubies and molten gold: from the western slopes of far-off California I have looked down upon the sun dipping into the wide Pacific amidst a riot of colour – but nothing like this! It is not always necessary to leave England in search of the strange and beautiful."

Crowland's blind Rector

A remarkable man lived at Crowland in the late 18th century. He was the Reverend Benson, Rector of the abbey church. It seems that he was born blind, but he was nevertheless a remarkable scholar, having been educated at Wadham College. With excellent commonsense, modest, very agreeable and entertaining in company, Mr. Benson was perfectly capable of conducting church services and would read the first lesson without the least hesitation. He took a small boy with him to the reading desk in case he should accidently make an error, but it was said he was never wrong. He even took over the services at another parish when the Rector there was indisposed. There it seems he performed his duties with astonishing elegance. A gentleman, ill in bed, asked to see the blind parson and could not resist asking him the secret of his success in the face of such a serious affliction and would he again officiate in that parish so that he might hear him. "Sir," replied the clergyman, "it is necessary for me to have my sermons written as it is for those that can see; but if it is possible as the weather is fair, I will oblige you."

On the following Saturday the blind man arose at 5 a.m. and walked with his little servant until breakfast, when he sent word to the gentleman who had been ill that he would deliver a sermon at his church that day. The listener later wrote that a better discourse in language or matter he had never heard; not did he ever hear the prayers uttered in a more edifying or engaging manner. The impressed listener had taken the Rector's little helper aged about 14 aside and asked him whether his master's sermon was new. "Perfectly so, sir" the boy replied. "I write all my master's discourses out for him; but this I never wrote, nor did he ever think of it until after he left you."

The astonished man said: "Your master told me that when he wants to refer to a passage in the Greek testament, he has taught you to read Greek so well as to understand it from your reading. "Ah, sir," replied the boy, "so he tells me but I don't understand a word of it." The boy was invited to read from a Greek testament, and read it so intelligibly that the listener perfectly understood the meaning of the author

Mr. Benson had lamented one of his greatest hardships was that of his inability to keep a good servant. His wages were but £80 a year and out of that amount he kept his predecessor's widow and daughter, "so that," said the worthy man, "as soon as I have taught one of my parishioners to read well and make tolerably master of my method, he must leave me to seek a more advantageous employment, and I have all the labour to go over again."

The blind gentleman met with a tragic end. He thought of his horse as he would of a good person. She had carried him safely to many places and brought him back home. One day after being put out to grass the animal broke a led and had to be put down. Mr. Benson was given another horse which did not have the abilities of his trusty old steed. One day he mounted the animal and at the same time it started at something and the clergyman fell heavily to the ground. The fall killed him after serving as faithful priest of Crowland for thirty years.

. . . and a blind Sexton

The following is an extract from a letter written by Mr. Robert Hardy in 1782 to his friend, a medical practitioner:

"Travelling from Spalding to Peterborough, I made Crowland abbey on my way. There I beheld the ruins of that once celebrated place which I think travellers will not have many years to view, it being almost entirely demolished.

"I walked about the churchyard and had much talk with the Sexton who was very merry, digging a grave. I found him a pleasant, intelligent, facetious fellow, and could not help being highly entertained with his humour and drollery. Afterwards he pointed to the cottage where his wife was who had the key of the church. When there, I congratulated her on having so cheerful a husband. She said indeed he was a very good man and a good scholar, as well as Sexton, that he had always been the easiest person in the world, excepting one year in his life during which period he continually fretted day and night. I asked the occasion and heard of his misfortune – loss of sight.

"Well, be thankful he is recovered and got well again!" "Yes sir," she said, "he is well to be sure but has never got the better of his blindness, nor has he been able to see for eighteen years past." "The woman astonished me. I enquired repeatedly if she really meant the man whom I saw digging the grave, for I had been prating with the poor fellow some considerable time and he never once lamented his loss of sight or even threw out the most distant hint of his being blind, but kept shovelling up the earth and talking with as much ease as it is possible to conceive, and without a murmer or complaint.

"It is a fact that the man had been Sexton at Crowland twenty-two years and had done the business of a Sexton seventeen years since his blindness ceased to distress him. It was occasioned by a cold he caught one severe winter when he was obliged to travel about in the snow, on foot, to many places in search of some person to officiate for a Mr. Benson, the gentleman who then had the living, and what is equally extraordinary, that very gentleman, too, was blind."

A tablet was erected in memory of the blind Sexton in the porch of Crowland abbey:

William Hill, Sexton of this parish, lost his sight by walking in snow when forty years of age, and yet he acquired all the faculties of those who met this malady in youth, his acuteness almost superseded his loss since he could walk in and about the town and could go in the churchyard, find each and every grave he was desired to point out. He died January 27th 1792, aged sixty-five. To record these singulat faculties, and their esteem, the parishioners erected this tablet in 1818.

Fridaybridge water tower

This conspicuous brick landmark between March and Wisbech was erected in 1894. It stands upon foundations more than thirty feet deep and is one-hundred-and-twelve feet high. The base walls are six feet nine inches thick. The tower is remarkably upright which is more than can be said of Fridaybridge church tower a short distance away which leans over and pulls the nave with it. A mast surmounting the water tower once beamed the monarch's Christmas message from Sandringham to the Commonwealth nations scattered throughout the world.

Rebuked the Queen

Few people kept their heads were they so foolhardy to rebuke the great Tudor Queen, Elizabeth the First. Christopher Tye did! He was Rector of Doddington-cum-March-cum-Benwick, at one time the largest parish in the county with 40,000 acres and the wealthiest living in the country. Tye wrote a great many masses in the reign of Henry the Eighth and composed Protestant hymns under Edward the Sixth. He was promoted music master by Mary Tudor and was royal organist to Queen Elizabeth. On one occasion his finger missed a note and the red-haired Queen rebuked him. The organist promptly retorted that her ears were out of tune! Christopher Tye wrote a tune known throughout Christendom "While Shepherds Watched Their Flocks By Night." He also composed the National Anthem, the tune in his day accompanying dancers. Centuries ago a resident of Doddington committed a great wrong. To remind him of his guilt a small hand was carved on a choir stall and painted red. Each year it was partly erased and when, at last, no trace of it remained, the person was completely absolved of guilt.

Hung by order of the Bishop

The drainage of the Fens and enclosure of common land introduced much hardship to inhabitants, relying as they did on their food supply of rabbits, hares, fish and wildfowl. Seeing their families deprived of food and ill for want of it, the men of Littleport got themselves together and ransacked the shops, then, made bold by success, armed themselves and marched upon Ely, holding the city to ransom at the point of punt guns mounted on a waggon. Troops from Bury St. Edmunds quelled the rioters who were put on trial. Seventy men were sent to prison, five were transported and five - the ringleaders - were hung in the shadow of the cathedral. No-one would lend a cart to take the men to the scaffold, so the bishop as Chief Magistrate, with a hard heart, paid five guineas for one. The bodies were committed to a communal grave at the rear of St. Mary's church, and a tablet commemorating the event attached to the church wall.

Bell, book and candle

In the fourteenth century St. Mary's church, Doddington was the scene of the full ecclesiatical curse, "bell, book and candle." It was directed against unknown felons who had purloined the bishop's cattle. A frightening affair, people kept themselves indoors during the procedure. A similar curse was threatened against Benwick for similar reasons.